REFLECTIVE JOURNAL

Based on the Gibbs' Cyclic Reflective Model

www.hand-crafted-media.co.uk/books

INTRODUCTION TO GIBBS' REFLECTIVE CYCLE

The Gibbs' Reflective Cycle is one of the most famous models of reflection using a cyclical process that guides you through six areas of reflection: description, feelings, evaluation, analysis, conclusion and action plan.

OVERVIEW

This model of reflection is named after its developer, Graham Gibbs, who in 1988 used it to bring a structured framework to the act of learning from experience. The cyclic nature of the model makes it ideal for reflecting upon experiences that are repeated – over six stages, it guides you to learn and plan from areas that went well and also from experiences that didn't go so well.

The six stages are outlined below:

1. **DESCRIPTION** – the starting point is to describe what happened in the experience under reflection.
2. **FEELINGS** – you then move on to describe your thoughts and feelings about the experience.
3. **EVALUATION** – attempt to work out what was both good and bad about the situation.
4. **ANALYSIS** – bring together your thoughts and reflections so far to try to make sense of what happened.
5. **CONCLUSION** – here you can describe what you have learned from the experience and also what you would do differently next time.
6. **ACTION PLAN** – this final section of the cycle allows you to work out a plan for how to deal with similar experiences moving forward, and also for more general changes that you think might work well, as a result of your reflection.

Remember that this is just one model of reflection and for some experiences, not all of the stages will be helpful for you – if you find this to be the case, then just concentrate on the stages that you do think will be helpful, but by thinking about each of the stages in relation to your experience, you are more likely to think critically and learn more from the experience.

THE MODEL

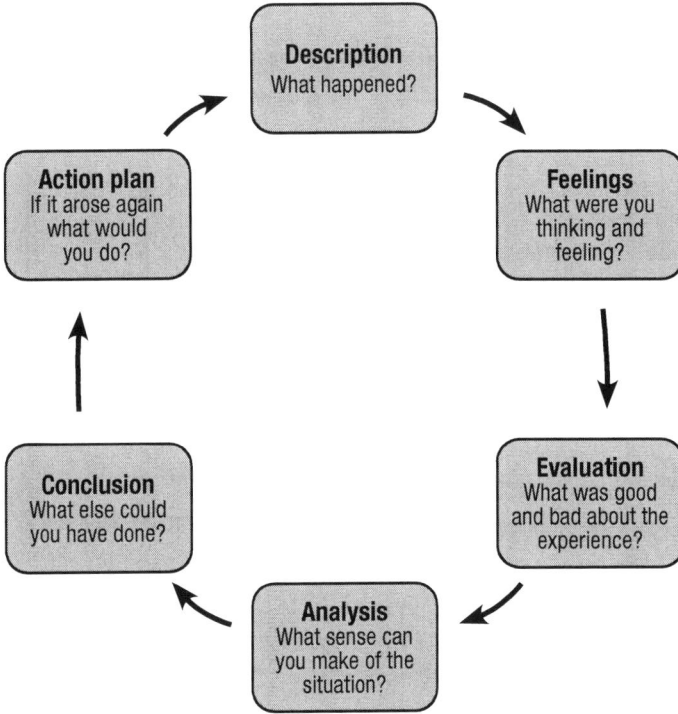

Gibbs' reflective cycle

This reflective cycle is a very good way to work through both a standalone experience or something that you go through on a frequent basis. An example of this might be for team meetings that you have on a regular basis – indeed Gibbs proposed from the outset that the model should be used for repeated situations – but it can be just as effective in a standalone situation but the outcomes from the action plan stage may look more general.

To work through each of the stages, there are a number of useful questions to ask yourself and consider, which are listed below. It is not necessary to answer them all for each of the stages, just use the ones that are useful for the particular experience that you are reflecting on. They may also prompt you to ask your own questions and these may well work better for you.

There is also an example entry for you to see how to put all of this into your journal.

1. DESCRIPTION

The starting point for your reflection is to describe what happened in detail in your particular experience. Remember that you are just describing the events of the experience – your feelings and further conclusions will come later.

Questions to ask:

- *What happened?*
- *When and where did it happen?*
- *Who was present?*
- *What did you and the other people do?*
- *What was the outcome of the situation?*
- *Why were you there?*
- *What did you want to happen?*

2. FEELINGS

Use this stage to explore how the experience made you feel, or any thoughts that you had during the situation – and how your thoughts and feelings may have impacted upon the situation.

Questions to ask:

- *What were you feeling during the situation?*
- *What were you feeling before and after the situation?*
- *What do you think other people were feeling about the situation?*
- *What do you think other people feel about the situation now?*
- *What were you thinking during the situation?*
- *What do you think about the situation now?*

3. EVALUATION

Use this stage to describe what worked well in the situation and also what didn't work so well. It is important to try to be as objective and honest as you possibly can and so that you can get the most from your reflection, focus on both the negative and the positive aspects from the situation, even if there was mainly only one of them – positive or negative.

Questions to ask:

- *What was good and bad about the experience?*
- *What went well?*
- *What didn't go so well?*
- *What did you and other people contribute to the situation (positively or negatively)?*

4. ANALYSIS

This is your opportunity to make sense of what happened during the experience, or to put it another way – to find the meaning from what happened based upon the details that you have described so far. You can do this by asking yourself why did this happen.

Questions to ask:
- *Why did things go well?*
- *Why didn't it go well?*
- *What sense can I make of the situation?*
- *What knowledge – my own or others (for example academic literature) can help me understand the situation?*

5. CONCLUSIONS

At this stage you can now make some conclusions from what happened and summarise what you have learnt and what you might do differently next time around. This should be a natural progression from what you set out in your previous stage.

Questions to ask:
- *What did I learn from this situation?*
- *How could this have been a more positive situation for everyone involved?*
- *What skills do I need to develop for me to handle a situation like this better?*
- *What else could I have done?*

6. ACTION PLAN

This is your opportunity for you to plan how you go about things in the future, what you would do differently and how you can make sure that you will make these changes. Sometimes, just the act of reflecting will be enough for you to move forward with any changes – but you can also use this stage to give yourself specific reminders or cues for the future.

Questions to ask:
- *If I had to do the same thing again, what would I do differently?*
- *How will I develop the required skills I need?*
- *How can I make sure that I can act differently next time?*

EXAMPLE JOURNAL ENTRY AND DIFFERENT DEPTHS OF REFLECTION

An example journal entry follows to show you how you can dive deep into a situation, but you can also keep things brief. The level of depth that you go into will be dependent upon the context and purpose of the reflection that you are undertaking – The Gibbs' model can be effective across all levels.

Best wishes for your reflections…!

Adapted from Gibbs G (1988). *Learning by Doing: A guide to teaching and learning methods.* Further Education Unit. Oxford Polytechnic: Oxford.

REF. TITLE: *Group work assignment*

1. DESCRIPTION   What happened?

We were put into a group of five on the course I am studying and given a written assignment that we had to complete together in a team. We decided to each work on a different area of the assignment and expected that we could just bring it all together into one coherent written piece of work, on the afternoon before the day of the assignment deadline.

However, when we all sat down with our written pieces it became obvious that there was no coherence to the final piece, as all of our writing styles were different and there was no consistency.

As a result we had to re-write most of the pieces again to bring them together into a coherent whole - so while we had all allowed sufficient time to write our individual pieces before the deadline, we hadn't taken into consideration a plan for when they were all brought together and what problems might have occurred from that. Three members of the team had to abandon their plans and we worked late into the night to make sure the piece was complete in time for the deadline.

2. FEELINGS   What were you thinking and feeling?

Before the deadline and we tried to bring all of our separate pieces together, I was feeling quite good about how we had divided the work up - and thought that it was going to work really well.

When I realised that it wasn't going to work and that more work was needed, I became quite frustrated and had felt little incentive to do any re-writing because I was certain it was going to work.

When people had to cancel their evening plans to do the re-writes, I felt quite guilty, but this gave me the incentive to get the work done faster. I'm glad that we did do the extra work to bring it all together.

3. EVALUATION   What was good and bad about the experience?

What worked well was that each member of the group wrote a good quality contribution in time for deadline - and when the team members cancelled their evening plans that did motivate us to work harder in the evening and helped contribute to the team's sense of work ethic.

What didn't work well was that we all assumed that we would write in the same way, or nobody foresaw that as an issue, and so the general time plan for the team failed.

6

DATE: 4th March

4. ANALYSIS — What sense can you make of the situation?

The reason that the division of work in the first place worked well was that everyone had a say in the areas that they wanted to work on - so it was playing to everyone's strengths. I have worked like this before and find that it makes sense for people to work on the areas that they feel best about.

Also, we thought that working this way would save us time in the long run and when it came to putting the final piece of work - however, in reality, it ended up costing us lots more time than we had anticipated because we didn't anticipate the impact of the different writing styles. This probably happened because we didn't properly plan and structure how we were going to write the sections and how they would come together.

Although we did well to play to each member's strengths, we fell in part to groupthink and none of us felt confident to be critical or speak out about the proposed plan of working and took it for granted that it would all be good because we all thought that we were good students.

We need to be aware of groupthink in the future to prevent this kind of thing from happening again.

5. CONCLUSION — What else could you have done?

There are two main takeaways from this situation that I have learnt. The first is that although we divided the work up well based upon our strengths, what we didn't take into account was a plan for how the finished piece would sound and feel in a complete form - also, none of us were able to see this is a potential issue when we were discussing the work - so we need to learn to challenge group decisions to make sure that they are sound and ensure that we are not falling into groupthink.

6. ACTION PLAN — If it arose again what would you do?

When working in a group next time, we can continue to divide the work up based upon people's strengths and this is also a good way to introduce the group, if we do not know each other. But we must ensure that we insist on planning out what our expectations are beforehand, potentially by:

- Writing an introduction together so that we all have a reference
- Be sure to challenge group decisions even if it feels uncomfortable, to make sure we haven't fallen for groupthink.

REF. TITLE:

1. DESCRIPTION What happened?

2. FEELINGS What were you thinking and feeling?

3. EVALUATION What was good and bad about the experience?

DATE:

4. ANALYSIS What sense can you make of the situation?

5. CONCLUSION What else could you have done?

6. ACTION PLAN If it arose again what would you do?

9

REF. TITLE:

1. DESCRIPTION What happened?

2. FEELINGS What were you thinking and feeling?

3. EVALUATION What was good and bad about the experience?

DATE:

4. ANALYSIS   What sense can you make of the situation?

5. CONCLUSION   What else could you have done?

6. ACTION PLAN   If it arose again what would you do?

REF. TITLE:

1. DESCRIPTION What happened?

2. FEELINGS What were you thinking and feeling?

3. EVALUATION What was good and bad about the experience?

DATE:

4. ANALYSIS   What sense can you make of the situation?

5. CONCLUSION   What else could you have done?

6. ACTION PLAN   If it arose again what would you do?

REF. TITLE:

1. DESCRIPTION What happened?

2. FEELINGS What were you thinking and feeling?

3. EVALUATION What was good and bad about the experience?

DATE:

4. ANALYSIS   What sense can you make of the situation?

5. CONCLUSION   What else could you have done?

6. ACTION PLAN   If it arose again what would you do?

REF. TITLE:

1. DESCRIPTION What happened?

2. FEELINGS What were you thinking and feeling?

3. EVALUATION What was good and bad about the experience?

16

DATE:

4. ANALYSIS   What sense can you make of the situation?

5. CONCLUSION   What else could you have done?

6. ACTION PLAN   If it arose again what would you do?

REF. TITLE:

1. DESCRIPTION What happened?

2. FEELINGS What were you thinking and feeling?

3. EVALUATION What was good and bad about the experience?

DATE:

4. ANALYSIS   What sense can you make of the situation?

5. CONCLUSION   What else could you have done?

6. ACTION PLAN   If it arose again what would you do?

REF. TITLE:

1. DESCRIPTION What happened?

2. FEELINGS What were you thinking and feeling?

3. EVALUATION What was good and bad about the experience?

DATE:

4. ANALYSIS   What sense can you make of the situation?

5. CONCLUSION   What else could you have done?

6. ACTION PLAN   If it arose again what would you do?

REF. TITLE:

1. DESCRIPTION What happened?

2. FEELINGS What were you thinking and feeling?

3. EVALUATION What was good and bad about the experience?

DATE:

4. ANALYSIS What sense can you make of the situation?

5. CONCLUSION What else could you have done?

6. ACTION PLAN If it arose again what would you do?

REF. TITLE:

1. DESCRIPTION What happened?

2. FEELINGS What were you thinking and feeling?

3. EVALUATION What was good and bad about the experience?

DATE:

4. ANALYSIS   What sense can you make of the situation?

5. CONCLUSION   What else could you have done?

6. ACTION PLAN   If it arose again what would you do?

REF. TITLE:

1. DESCRIPTION What happened?

2. FEELINGS What were you thinking and feeling?

3. EVALUATION What was good and bad about the experience?

DATE:

4. ANALYSIS   What sense can you make of the situation?

5. CONCLUSION   What else could you have done?

6. ACTION PLAN   If it arose again what would you do?

REF. TITLE:

1. DESCRIPTION What happened?

2. FEELINGS What were you thinking and feeling?

3. EVALUATION What was good and bad about the experience?

DATE:

4. ANALYSIS   What sense can you make of the situation?

5. CONCLUSION   What else could you have done?

6. ACTION PLAN   If it arose again what would you do?

REF. TITLE:

1. DESCRIPTION What happened?

2. FEELINGS What were you thinking and feeling?

3. EVALUATION What was good and bad about the experience?

DATE:

4. ANALYSIS What sense can you make of the situation?

5. CONCLUSION What else could you have done?

6. ACTION PLAN If it arose again what would you do?

REF. TITLE:

1. DESCRIPTION What happened?

2. FEELINGS What were you thinking and feeling?

3. EVALUATION What was good and bad about the experience?

DATE:

4. ANALYSIS What sense can you make of the situation?

5. CONCLUSION What else could you have done?

6. ACTION PLAN If it arose again what would you do?

REF. TITLE:

1. DESCRIPTION What happened?

2. FEELINGS What were you thinking and feeling?

3. EVALUATION What was good and bad about the experience?

DATE:

4. ANALYSIS What sense can you make of the situation?

5. CONCLUSION What else could you have done?

6. ACTION PLAN If it arose again what would you do?

REF. TITLE:

1. DESCRIPTION What happened?

2. FEELINGS What were you thinking and feeling?

3. EVALUATION What was good and bad about the experience?

DATE:

4. ANALYSIS What sense can you make of the situation?

5. CONCLUSION What else could you have done?

6. ACTION PLAN If it arose again what would you do?

REF. TITLE:

1. DESCRIPTION What happened?

2. FEELINGS What were you thinking and feeling?

3. EVALUATION What was good and bad about the experience?

DATE:

4. ANALYSIS   What sense can you make of the situation?

5. CONCLUSION   What else could you have done?

6. ACTION PLAN   If it arose again what would you do?

REF. TITLE:

1. DESCRIPTION What happened?

2. FEELINGS What were you thinking and feeling?

3. EVALUATION What was good and bad about the experience?

DATE:

4. ANALYSIS   What sense can you make of the situation?

5. CONCLUSION   What else could you have done?

6. ACTION PLAN   If it arose again what would you do?

REF. TITLE:

1. DESCRIPTION What happened?

2. FEELINGS What were you thinking and feeling?

3. EVALUATION What was good and bad about the experience?

DATE:

4. ANALYSIS   What sense can you make of the situation?

5. CONCLUSION   What else could you have done?

6. ACTION PLAN   If it arose again what would you do?

REF. TITLE:

1. DESCRIPTION What happened?

2. FEELINGS What were you thinking and feeling?

3. EVALUATION What was good and bad about the experience?

DATE:

4. ANALYSIS What sense can you make of the situation?

5. CONCLUSION What else could you have done?

6. ACTION PLAN If it arose again what would you do?

REF. TITLE:

1. DESCRIPTION What happened?

2. FEELINGS What were you thinking and feeling?

3. EVALUATION What was good and bad about the experience?

DATE:

4. ANALYSIS What sense can you make of the situation?

5. CONCLUSION What else could you have done?

6. ACTION PLAN If it arose again what would you do?

REF. TITLE:

1. DESCRIPTION What happened?

2. FEELINGS What were you thinking and feeling?

3. EVALUATION What was good and bad about the experience?

DATE:

4. ANALYSIS What sense can you make of the situation?

5. CONCLUSION What else could you have done?

6. ACTION PLAN If it arose again what would you do?

REF. TITLE:

1. DESCRIPTION What happened?

2. FEELINGS What were you thinking and feeling?

3. EVALUATION What was good and bad about the experience?

DATE:

4. ANALYSIS   What sense can you make of the situation?

5. CONCLUSION   What else could you have done?

6. ACTION PLAN   If it arose again what would you do?

REF. TITLE:

1. DESCRIPTION What happened?

2. FEELINGS What were you thinking and feeling?

3. EVALUATION What was good and bad about the experience?

DATE:

4. ANALYSIS — What sense can you make of the situation?

5. CONCLUSION — What else could you have done?

6. ACTION PLAN — If it arose again what would you do?

REF. TITLE:

1. DESCRIPTION What happened?

2. FEELINGS What were you thinking and feeling?

3. EVALUATION What was good and bad about the experience?

DATE:

4. ANALYSIS What sense can you make of the situation?

5. CONCLUSION What else could you have done?

6. ACTION PLAN If it arose again what would you do?

REF. TITLE:

1. DESCRIPTION What happened?

2. FEELINGS What were you thinking and feeling?

3. EVALUATION What was good and bad about the experience?

DATE:

4. ANALYSIS What sense can you make of the situation?

5. CONCLUSION What else could you have done?

6. ACTION PLAN If it arose again what would you do?

REF. TITLE:

1. DESCRIPTION What happened?

2. FEELINGS What were you thinking and feeling?

3. EVALUATION What was good and bad about the experience?

DATE:

4. ANALYSIS   What sense can you make of the situation?

5. CONCLUSION   What else could you have done?

6. ACTION PLAN   If it arose again what would you do?

REF. TITLE:

1. DESCRIPTION What happened?

2. FEELINGS What were you thinking and feeling?

3. EVALUATION What was good and bad about the experience?

DATE:

4. ANALYSIS   What sense can you make of the situation?

5. CONCLUSION   What else could you have done?

6. ACTION PLAN   If it arose again what would you do?

REF. TITLE:

1. DESCRIPTION What happened?

2. FEELINGS What were you thinking and feeling?

3. EVALUATION What was good and bad about the experience?

DATE:

4. ANALYSIS   What sense can you make of the situation?

5. CONCLUSION   What else could you have done?

6. ACTION PLAN   If it arose again what would you do?

REF. TITLE:

1. DESCRIPTION What happened?

2. FEELINGS What were you thinking and feeling?

3. EVALUATION What was good and bad about the experience?

DATE:

4. ANALYSIS What sense can you make of the situation?

5. CONCLUSION What else could you have done?

6. ACTION PLAN If it arose again what would you do?

REF. TITLE:

1. DESCRIPTION What happened?

2. FEELINGS What were you thinking and feeling?

3. EVALUATION What was good and bad about the experience?

DATE:

4. ANALYSIS What sense can you make of the situation?

5. CONCLUSION What else could you have done?

6. ACTION PLAN If it arose again what would you do?

REF. TITLE:

1. DESCRIPTION What happened?

2. FEELINGS What were you thinking and feeling?

3. EVALUATION What was good and bad about the experience?

DATE:

4. ANALYSIS What sense can you make of the situation?

5. CONCLUSION What else could you have done?

6. ACTION PLAN If it arose again what would you do?

REF. TITLE:

1. DESCRIPTION What happened?

2. FEELINGS What were you thinking and feeling?

3. EVALUATION What was good and bad about the experience?

DATE:

4. ANALYSIS What sense can you make of the situation?

5. CONCLUSION What else could you have done?

6. ACTION PLAN If it arose again what would you do?

REF. TITLE:

1. DESCRIPTION What happened?

2. FEELINGS What were you thinking and feeling?

3. EVALUATION What was good and bad about the experience?

DATE:

4. ANALYSIS   What sense can you make of the situation?

5. CONCLUSION   What else could you have done?

6. ACTION PLAN   If it arose again what would you do?

REF. TITLE:

1. DESCRIPTION What happened?

2. FEELINGS What were you thinking and feeling?

3. EVALUATION What was good and bad about the experience?

DATE:

4. ANALYSIS What sense can you make of the situation?

5. CONCLUSION What else could you have done?

6. ACTION PLAN If it arose again what would you do?

REF. TITLE:

1. DESCRIPTION What happened?

2. FEELINGS What were you thinking and feeling?

3. EVALUATION What was good and bad about the experience?

DATE:

4. ANALYSIS What sense can you make of the situation?

5. CONCLUSION What else could you have done?

6. ACTION PLAN If it arose again what would you do?

REF. TITLE:

1. DESCRIPTION What happened?

2. FEELINGS What were you thinking and feeling?

3. EVALUATION What was good and bad about the experience?

DATE:

4. ANALYSIS   What sense can you make of the situation?

5. CONCLUSION   What else could you have done?

6. ACTION PLAN   If it arose again what would you do?

REF. TITLE:

1. DESCRIPTION What happened?

2. FEELINGS What were you thinking and feeling?

3. EVALUATION What was good and bad about the experience?

DATE:

4. ANALYSIS What sense can you make of the situation?

5. CONCLUSION What else could you have done?

6. ACTION PLAN If it arose again what would you do?

REF. TITLE:

1. DESCRIPTION What happened?

2. FEELINGS What were you thinking and feeling?

3. EVALUATION What was good and bad about the experience?

DATE:

4. ANALYSIS   What sense can you make of the situation?

5. CONCLUSION   What else could you have done?

6. ACTION PLAN   If it arose again what would you do?

REF. TITLE:

1. DESCRIPTION What happened?

2. FEELINGS What were you thinking and feeling?

3. EVALUATION What was good and bad about the experience?

DATE:

4. ANALYSIS   What sense can you make of the situation?

5. CONCLUSION   What else could you have done?

6. ACTION PLAN   If it arose again what would you do?

REF. TITLE:

1. DESCRIPTION What happened?

2. FEELINGS What were you thinking and feeling?

3. EVALUATION What was good and bad about the experience?

DATE:

4. ANALYSIS What sense can you make of the situation?

5. CONCLUSION What else could you have done?

6. ACTION PLAN If it arose again what would you do?

REF. TITLE:

1. DESCRIPTION What happened?

2. FEELINGS What were you thinking and feeling?

3. EVALUATION What was good and bad about the experience?

DATE:

4. ANALYSIS What sense can you make of the situation?

5. CONCLUSION What else could you have done?

6. ACTION PLAN If it arose again what would you do?

REF. TITLE:

1. DESCRIPTION What happened?

2. FEELINGS What were you thinking and feeling?

3. EVALUATION What was good and bad about the experience?

DATE:

4. ANALYSIS What sense can you make of the situation?

5. CONCLUSION What else could you have done?

6. ACTION PLAN If it arose again what would you do?

REF. TITLE:

1. DESCRIPTION What happened?

2. FEELINGS What were you thinking and feeling?

3. EVALUATION What was good and bad about the experience?

DATE:

4. ANALYSIS What sense can you make of the situation?

5. CONCLUSION What else could you have done?

6. ACTION PLAN If it arose again what would you do?

REF. TITLE:

1. DESCRIPTION What happened?

2. FEELINGS What were you thinking and feeling?

3. EVALUATION What was good and bad about the experience?

DATE:

4. ANALYSIS What sense can you make of the situation?

5. CONCLUSION What else could you have done?

6. ACTION PLAN If it arose again what would you do?

REF. TITLE:

1. DESCRIPTION What happened?

2. FEELINGS What were you thinking and feeling?

3. EVALUATION What was good and bad about the experience?

DATE:

4. ANALYSIS   What sense can you make of the situation?

5. CONCLUSION   What else could you have done?

6. ACTION PLAN   If it arose again what would you do?

REF. TITLE:

1. DESCRIPTION What happened?

2. FEELINGS What were you thinking and feeling?

3. EVALUATION What was good and bad about the experience?

DATE:

4. ANALYSIS   What sense can you make of the situation?

5. CONCLUSION   What else could you have done?

6. ACTION PLAN   If it arose again what would you do?

REF. TITLE:

1. DESCRIPTION What happened?

2. FEELINGS What were you thinking and feeling?

3. EVALUATION What was good and bad about the experience?

DATE:

4. ANALYSIS What sense can you make of the situation?

5. CONCLUSION What else could you have done?

6. ACTION PLAN If it arose again what would you do?

REF. TITLE:

1. DESCRIPTION What happened?

2. FEELINGS What were you thinking and feeling?

3. EVALUATION What was good and bad about the experience?

DATE:

4. ANALYSIS What sense can you make of the situation?

5. CONCLUSION What else could you have done?

6. ACTION PLAN If it arose again what would you do?

REF. TITLE:

1. DESCRIPTION What happened?

2. FEELINGS What were you thinking and feeling?

3. EVALUATION What was good and bad about the experience?

DATE:

4. ANALYSIS   What sense can you make of the situation?

5. CONCLUSION   What else could you have done?

6. ACTION PLAN   If it arose again what would you do?

REF. TITLE:

1. DESCRIPTION What happened?

2. FEELINGS What were you thinking and feeling?

3. EVALUATION What was good and bad about the experience?

DATE:

4. ANALYSIS What sense can you make of the situation?

5. CONCLUSION What else could you have done?

6. ACTION PLAN If it arose again what would you do?

Printed in Great Britain
by Amazon